D1560324

I WANT TO KNOW

Are Unicorns Real?

Portia Summers and
Dana Meachen Rau

Enslow Publishing
101 W. 23rd Street
Suite 240
New York, NY 10011
USA

enslow.com

Published in 2017 by Enslow Publishing, LLC
101 W. 23rd Street, Suite 240, New York, NY 10011

Library of Congress Cataloging-in-Publication Data

Names: Summers, Portia.
Title: Are unicorns real? / Portia Summers and Dana Meachen Rau.
Description: New York, NY : Enslow Publishing, 2017. | Series: I want to know| Includes bibliographical references and index.
Identifiers: LCCN 2016024762| ISBN 9780766082502 (library bound) | ISBN 9780766082489 (pbk.) | ISBN 9780766082496 (6-pack)
Subjects: LCSH: Unicorns—Juvenile literature.
Classification: LCC GR830.U6 S86 2017 | DDC 398.24/54—dc23
LC record available at https://lccn.loc.gov/2016024762

Printed in China

To Our Readers: We have done our best to make sure all websites in this book were active and appropriate when we went to press. However, the author and the publisher have no control over and assume no liability for the material available on those websites or on any websites they may link to. Any comments or suggestions can be sent by email to customerservice@enslow.com.

Photo Credits: Cover © iStockphoto.com/CoreyFord pp. 3, 26 Lucy von Held/Blend Images/Getty Images; p. 4 Marben/Shutterstock.com; p. 5 GraphicaArtis/Archive Photos/Getty Images; p. 6 Colors Hunter - Chasseur de Couleurs/Moment/Getty Images; pp. 7, 23 Florilegius/SSPL/Getty Images; p. 9 Mondadori Portfolio/Getty Images; pp. 10, 22 DEA/Archivio J. Lange/De Agostini/Getty Images; p. 11 Philip and Elizabeth De Bay/Corbis Historical/Getty Images; p. 12 Kachelhoffer Clement/Corbis Historical/Getty Images; p. 13 ©Warner Bros./Courtesy Everett Collection; p. 14 Hubert Fanthomme/Paris Match/Getty Images; p. 15 Print Collector/Hulton Archive/Getty Images; pp. 17, 20 Science & Society Picture Library/SSPL/Getty Images; p. 18 Universal History Archive/Universal Images Group/Getty Images; p. 19 Lake Superior State University, Sault Ste. Marie, Mich.; p. 24 Flip Nicklin/Minden Pictures/SuperStock; p. 25 DEA/A. Dagli Orti/De Agostini Picture Library/Getty Images.

Contents

Chapter 1

A Horse of a Different Color

Imagine taking a walk in the woods. Suddenly, you notice a large, white animal through the trees. It is bent down, drinking from the stream. As you get closer, you can see it has the body of a horse. It raises its face, and you can see a single horn sticking out of its forehead. Standing before you is a unicorn!

Imagine That!

There are seven very famous unicorn **tapestries** from the Middle Ages. These can be seen at the Cloisters, part of the Metropolitan Museum of Art, in New York City.

A National Symbol

The unicorn is part of the coat of arms of the British royal family. It is also the national symbol of Scotland. The unicorn is a common decoration in the United Kingdom. Unicorns can be found on buildings, as statues in parks, and even on the front gate of Buckingham Palace!

Part Fantasy, Part History

Throughout history, people have told many stories about unicorns. In some stories, these animals are gentle, pure, and loving. In other tales, unicorns are fierce, strong, and fast. They like to be alone and are impossible to catch. Reports of these creatures came from India, Africa, Asia, and across Europe. Travelers shared stories of unicorns, which helped the legend spread.

Mythical Monsters

Myths are filled with strange creatures. A hippogriff is part horse and part eagle. A sphinx has a lion's body and a human head. Centaurs have the lower body of a horse but the head and upper body of a

This bestiary shows a basilisk (2), a phoenix (3), a dragon (5), and a unicorn (4).

man. A phoenix is a bird that bursts into flames and dies, and then is reborn from the ashes. Gryffins have the body of a lion but the head and front talons of an eagle. A basilisk is part chicken and part snake. Unicorns aren't nearly as strange. They have the body of a horse, the cloven feet and beard of a goat, and a single, long horn. It was easy for many people to believe in unicorns, even if they had never seen one.

Chapter 2

· · · · · · · · · · · ·

Across the World, a Legend Arises

The unicorn as we know it today arose in Europe during the Middle Ages, in the time of castles, kings, and knights. At that time, they were so popular that they made their way into tapestries, artwork, and books. But these were not the first unicorns. Unicorn stories started about 5,000 years ago.

Asian Unicorns

The Chinese tell of the *qilin* [CHEE-lin]. A qilin (right) had the body of a deer, the head of a lion, and one horn. Some stories said it had green scales. The qilin was a

gentle creature that would not hurt other living things and could walk on grass without crushing the blades. The qilin and its Japanese cousin, the *kirin*, foretold the births and deaths of royal family members. It is said that the mother of the great philosopher Confucius was visited by a qilin before he was born.

This 15th-century statue of a qilin is in the Imperial garden (Yuhuayuan), in the Forbidden City, Beijing, China.

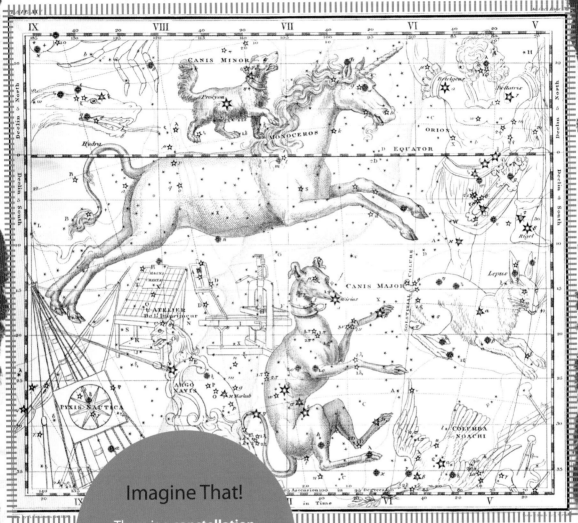

Imagine That!

There is a **constellation** of stars called Monocerus. Ancient astronomers thought the group of stars looked like a unicorn.

Ancient Greece and Rome

During the 5th century BCE, a Greek doctor named Ctesias [TEE-she-us] wrote about unicorns. He described a one-horned animal living in India. Two hundred years

Pliny the Elder

later, a Roman scholar called Pliny the Elder wrote a book called *Natural History*. This was one of the very first encyclopedias. In it, he described an animal of impossible strength with a horse's body, the head of a **stag**, the feet of an elephant, and a single black horn coming out of its forehead. It is clear to us today that Pliny and Ctesias were not describing a mythical unicorn but, instead, a rhinoceros.

Unicorns Today

The unicorn legend has not died. Unicorns are depicted in many books, songs, films, and television shows. They have been made into paintings, stuffed animals, decor, and characters on cartoons. They are often considered symbols of royalty. Unlike the unicorns of old, unicorns today can be brightly colored, be gentle or have attitude, or even be funny. Rapidash the Pokemon is a unicorn. Many characters on *My Little Pony* are unicorns. World famous wizard Harry Potter even had a single unicorn hair at the center of his wand that gave it power!

Unicorns of the Middle East

Islamic tradition tells of a creature called the *al-mi'raj* [AL-mii-raahg], which was a large yellow rabbit with a long, black, spiraling horn on its forehead. This was no harmless beast, however. It was very territorial and was said to kill trespassers with its horn. The *karkadann* [kar-ka-DANN] was a unicorn from Persian stories. This creature was said to resemble a hippopotamus. Like the al-mi'raj, the karkadann battled other animals with its sharp horn on deserts and grasslands.

The legend of the unicorn made its way into paintings, tapestries, bestiaries, and other works of art throughout history across the world, but especially in Europe.

Unicorns in the Bible

Early Bibles also mention unicorns. The Old Testament of the Bible is translated from Hebrew. This holy book told of a strong, large animal with a horn. The Hebrew word was *re'em*, which was translated into the Greek as *monoceros*, which means "one horned beast." Later, the word became *unicornis*. Many believed in unicorns because they were written about in these early Bibles.

Imagine That!

During the Middle Ages, it was popular for educated men to create **bestiaries**, which were books that contained all the information on the animals of the world that could be collected. Bestiaries often contained information on animals both real and imaginary.

Belief in the unicorn lasted for a very long time. A scientist in the early 1800s, however, claimed unicorns were an **impossibility**, meaning they couldn't be real. He said a one-horned creature like a unicorn could not exist because of the way bones grow in similar animals. As myth and legend gave way to science as a way of explaining the world, fewer and fewer people believed in unicorns.

Chapter 3

· · · · · · · · · · · · ·

Miraculous, Magical Horns

Of course, it is the horn that makes the unicorn **unique**. And it was said that the unicorn's horn had special powers. Some said the creature could dip its horn into a river and **purify** the water. Others thought the horn was powerful protection against poison. Unicorn horns were highly wanted for this reason.

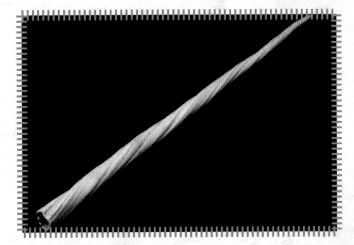

Horns such as this narwhal tusk were often sold for their supposed magical and healing properties.

To Catch a Unicorn

Some tales described unicorns as quick, strong, and dangerous to fight. They used their horns like swords, stabbing hunters who tried to catch them. According to myths, only a **virtuous** girl could catch a unicorn.

Imagine That!

A unicorn horn is called an **alicorn**. It was considered a powerful medicine that could cure anything from measles to fever to the plague.

A Modern-Day Unicorn Hunt

Lake Superior State University in Sault Ste Marie, Michigan, issues permits to unicorn **questers**, or hunters. Anyone interested in the quest can be given a permit and search for unicorns in the woods.

The Department of Natural Unicorns at the university recommends bringing the following items in your questing kit:

- A one-ounce bottle of Unicorn Lure
- A pair of scissors
- A large envelope
- One airmail stamp
- A nail clipper (with file)
- One horse comb
- A small bottle of hoof and horn polish
- A pair of hoof trimmers

ISSUED BY THE DEPARTMENT OF NATURAL UNICORNS OF THE UNICORN HUNTERS OF LAKE SUPERIOR STATE UNIVERSITY

Questing UNICORN LICENSE

Know Ye by these presents that this License, good for a lifetime & beyond except Valentine's Day, non-transferable, non-negotiable (once a member, always a member) is herewith issued to

who has been examined on the regulations of Unicorn Questing and found wanting to hunt unicorns and is therefore entitled to do so, both on the Planet Earth and elsewhere, within specifications, reules & misinterpretations as printed on this paper. Banded unicorns should be reported to the Director, police or D.A.R. Horn measurements as well as bearings on nearby virgins should be charted and notorized

Peter Thomas

DIRECTOR. Dept. of Natural Unicorns

DATE:

Design by MINGE

License reviewed by Wildlife Division, Dept. of Natural Resources of the State of Michigan. Final approval pending.

February, 1984
No. 34.601

LAKE SUPERIOR STATE UNIVERSITY

650 W. Easterday Avenue, Sault Ste. Marie, Michigan 49783 Phone: 1-888-800-LSSU Web: http://www.lssu.edu

So, hunters would bring a young girl into the woods with them. In these stories, the unicorn would come out of the woods to see her, and then the hunter could catch it.

Using Unicorn Horn

During the Middle Ages, horns sold as "unicorn" horns could fetch a high price. The wealthy made them into drinking cups, hoping to check for poison in their drinks. **Apothecaries** used ground up "unicorn" horn to make medicines. They claimed that medicine with unicorn horn could cure someone who had been poisoned.

This cup, from the 1700s, was supposedly made from unicorn horn.

Chapter 4

· · · · · · · · · · · ·

One-Horned Oddities

There are many stories from all over the world about unicorns. From Europe to Asia, Africa, India, and even the Americas, people told stories about unicorns and sought them out for their magical powers. For hundreds of years, many people used what they thought were unicorn horns in medicines, in crafts, and for protection against curses and poisons. But if unicorns weren't real, where did these tales come from? What made them so common in cultures across the globe? And what kind of horns were being used?

Natural Explanations

An oryx is a type of antelope that lives in Africa. It has two horns, but perhaps travellers saw an oryx from the side or from far away and thought it had one horn instead. Also, it is likely that many travellers, such as Marco Polo, saw a rhinoceros and considered it to be a unicorn.

Perhaps people saw an oryx (or a similar creature) from a distance and mistook it for the legendary unicorn.

An Ancient Unicorn

The elasmotherium was an ice age wooly rhinoceros that lived in Siberia over 30,000 years ago. Scientists have uncovered many fossils of this creature and suspect that it might have been the inspiration for the unicorn legend, since it is likely that these creatures lived at the same time as humans.

Unicorn of the Sea

While the horns sold during the Middle Ages were not unicorn horns, they did belong to one-horned creatures. A **narwhal** is a type of whale that lives in cold arctic waters. It has a single tusk growing out of its upper jaw that is actually a tooth. Sailors and fishermen found these horns on beaches or killed narwhals for their horns. The horn looked like the ones described in unicorn stories.

Scientists believe the male narwhal's long tusk is used to detect differences in the temperature and chemical composition of the water in which it lives.

Despite never having been scientifically proven, the legend of the
unicorn lives on today.

Unearthly Unicorns

Maybe unicorns did exist at one time. After all, many strange creatures on Earth have gone extinct. There are also animals that are born different than the rest of their kind. It is possible travellers saw a creature with one horn instead of two.

Think of all the strange creatures you see today. Giraffes with long necks, elephants with snakelike noses and tusks, alligators with scales and rows of teeth. What's so strange about a horse with one horn?

Words to Know

alicorn A unicorn's horn.

apothecary A person who made and sold medicine during the Middle Ages.

bestiary An encyclopedia that cataloged the beasts of nature.

constellation A pattern of stars.

impossibility Something that is impossible.

myth A story people tell to explain the past or describe unbelievable creatures or events.

narwhal A whale that lives in cold arctic waters and has a long tusk coming from its forehead.

purify To cleanse.

quester Hunter.

stag A male deer.

tapestry A heavy cloth with pictures woven into it.

unique Unlike anything else.

virtuous Moral, well-behaved, and righteous.

Further Reading

Books:

DK Publishing. *Children's Book of Mythical Beasts and Magical Monsters*. New York, NY: Penguin Random House, 2011.

Jeffery, Gary, and Dheeraj Verma. *Unicorns* (Graphic Mythical Creatures). New York, NY: Gareth Stevens Publishing, 2012.

Scamander, Newt. *Fantastic Beasts and Where to Find Them* (Harry Potter). New York, NY: Arthur A. Levine Books, 2015.

West, David, and Anita Ganeri. *The Illustrated Guide to Mythical Creatures*. St. Louis, MO: Hammond Books, 2009.

Websites:

All About Unicorns

www.allaboutunicorns.com

Read more about the legendary unicorn.

Lake Superior State University

www.lssu.edu/banished/uh_about.php

Learn about the regulations of unicorn questing and get a license!

National Geographic Kids

kids.nationalgeographic.com/explore/monster-myths/

Learn about myths that are actually based in fact!

Index